PRAISE FOR MENTORS 101

"With all the actionable steps and resources it contains, *Mentors 101* isn't just a book, it's an amazing tool; one that's going to save you years of trial and error! *Mentors 101* is a fantastic book with lots of fun stories, where Mathieu Fortin proves the world that finding a mentor doesn't have to be a hassle."

—MARTIN LATULIPPE
Founder, Académie ZEROLIMITE, International
Speaker, and four-time Bestselling Author

MENTORS 101

*How to Get a Mentor
to Help You Make Your
Dreams Come True*

MATHIEU FORTIN

CONTENTS

CONTENTS

INTRODUCTION

This is a book that I've wanted to write for a little while now—in fact, it's probably one that I would've needed myself when I started my entrepreneurial journey a few years ago.

And while this is a book in which you'll find a lot of valuable information on how to find the right mentor for your needs and how to leverage their experience to shorten your learning curve, it's definitely not going to teach you how to have someone else do all the work for you. If that's what you're looking for, then you've got the wrong book.

Because let's be clear. Having a mentor doesn't mean that you won't have to roll up your sleeves and get your hands dirty every once in a while. Nor does it guarantee you any kind of success whatsoever.

However, if you are willing to put in the efforts and make your success your number one priority, then I think a mentor can definitely come in pretty handy.

But before we jump into the nitty-gritty stuff, I'd like to properly introduce myself.

You probably already know this by now, but my name is Mathieu Fortin, and I'm a 20-year-old Canadian author and entrepreneur.

I bet you'd love to hear one of those crazy success stories hyped up in the media and on the internet, but the truth is; I'm just like you. I grew up in a middle-class family—living a decent life with loving parents. And for the better part of my childhood, I'd say I was just your average kid. I did okay in school, stayed out of trouble as much as possible, and rode my bike on the weekends with my friends.

In fact, it's not until I was about 14 years old that my personal development addiction began. I remember it like it was yesterday. At home, my mom kept this huge bookshelf filled with a bunch of personal development and business books—hundreds of them, literally.

Being a big car guy at heart, maybe I was simply looking for a way to eventually be able to buy all the cars I wanted. Or maybe my fascination grew because of the catchy titles lined up on the shelves, like *Think and Grow Rich* or *How to Be Wildly Wealthy FAST*. Whatever the reason, as soon as I started reading, I was hooked.

So much so that my interest for school soon started to slip away. The more books I read, the more I felt like I didn't belong in the traditional 9-to-5 path. You know, the "go to school, get a degree, find yourself a high-paying job and retire at 65" kind of path everyone seems to be hyping up? It just didn't really make any sense to me.

I wanted something more. I wanted to be an entrepreneur.

Therefore, when I turned sixteen, I decided to start my first online business—I had read a few books on how people were able to make millions of dollars online using their passion and a few marketing tricks. And quite frankly, this whole idea of making money while I was asleep seemed pretty clever to me, so I thought I'd give it a shot.

Three weeks later, my first blog was up and running. I still remember clicking the "Publish" button for the first time; I was terrified, and yet, so excited at the same time. All in all, I think I got three visits on my website that day. One was my dad, and the two others came from my own computer. But hey; you've got to start somewhere, right?

Within a year, things escalated for me. I started my second blog, sold the first one and met a ton of new people in the process—including my first real mentor.

Up until then, I had never really experienced what it was like to have a real two-way mentor-mentee relationship. I mean, I was reading books and all that stuff, so I guess I did have some influencers to look up to, but that was pretty much it.

Now, for the first time in my life, I had found someone willing to personally guide me through my inquiries and help me achieve my goals. And although I didn't realize it at the time, this was going to become my ticket to an even brighter future.

In fact, I think that being able to observe and learn directly from someone who already had the kind of success I wanted has made all the difference in the world for me. I mean, aside from the opportunities themselves, this relationship gave me a strong foundation of knowledge and wisdom on which I can now build anything I want.

That's true from a business standpoint, but also in life in general. What you can learn directly from another person goes way beyond anything you could ever draw from a book or an article.

I guess that's what you would call learning by osmosis. And to be honest, I think I've probably learned more in four years alongside my mentors than I have in eleven years sitting in a classroom. It's that simple.

And I'm not saying this to throw the blame on our educational system or anything; it's just the truth. Unfortunately, the things that often matter the most aren't taught in school these days.

Besides, we live in an era where everyone and their dog is talking about the importance of keeping a positive attitude, staying consistent and taking action. These are great, don't get me wrong, but when it comes to success, I truly believe that a big chunk of the equation lies in proper mentorship.

So, my goal with this book is to not only answer your questions, but also to help you find the right mentor for your needs. And although I have been through the whole process quite a few times myself, I feel like my vision alone wouldn't be enough to provide you with everything there is to know about mentors.

For that reason, I've decided to team up with six successful entrepreneurs to exchange on the subject and give those reflections a little more perspective—making the book you're holding right now a distillation of all these different visions.

Among these people, you'll find James Arthur Ray, *Inc. 500* entrepreneur and *New York Times* bestselling author that you've probably seen in the movie *The Secret*; Dave Ruel, serial entrepreneur and former bodybuilder who has made over $16 million online since he started in 2007; Pejman Ghadimi, author of the international bestseller *Third Circle Theory* and founder of *Secret Entourage*; Stephanie Nickolich, serial entrepreneur from the U.S. who's now making a killing with her coaching business; Doug Sandler, host of *The Nice Guys on Business* podcast and author of *Nice Guys*

Finish First; and Gerard Adams, co-founder of *Elite Daily* and self-made millionaire.

Together, the lessons they're going to share with you have the power to save you thousands of dollars and years of trial and error. But in order to make the most of that knowledge, you've got to be willing to leave your ego behind and become an apprentice. Let's be clear.

You'll find that each chapter of this book is addressing a specific question, providing you with a variety of relevant stories and anecdotes along the way.

Near the end of the book, you'll notice that I've also included two bonus interviews; one with Caleb Maddix, and the other with Sandy Forster. I'm sure you'll love all the empowering wisdom they have to share.

And of course, if at any given point throughout the book you want to learn more about one of the featured guests, you can always refer to the *Biographies* section at the end of the book.

With that being said, I truly hope that all these visions put together will provide you with the guidance and the actionable resources you need to find the right mentor for your needs. That's my goal with this book, and I'm really excited for you to dive in; so, let's get started!

Chapter 1

WHAT WOULD YOUR DEFINITION OF A MENTOR BE?

While this might sound like an obvious one, I think it would be a big mistake to overlook the importance of really understanding what we're dealing with, especially in this situation. Humans like to assume things; we like to take shortcuts, that's how our brain is wired. But let me ask you this; if you had to write it down explicitly, what would your definition of a mentor be?

Easier said than done, right? But in order to find something, you've got to know exactly what you're looking for. So, that's the question I asked our six guests right off the bat.

The first person to answer was Doug Sandler.

"A mentor would be somebody that can listen with an open heart and open mind, and provide advice to someone that is considerably less experienced than him in a certain field," he said. "To me, that would be the foundation of a good mentor-mentee relationship.

"And looking at it from my true world experience, I think that if somebody is reaching out to me asking for advice, it's probably because they feel like I'm in a position where I should be able to help them. So yeah, in a nutshell, I think a mentor is a person who is consistently in a position of being able to provide advice."

Now, for many reasons, this makes a lot of sense to me. Because, like Doug, I think a mentor should be someone who understands your present situation. Not only that, but it should also be someone who has already been where you want to be and done what you want to do.

And while Dave Ruel's perception of mentorship shares that same fundamental premise, it also highlights the fact that not all mentor-mentee relationships have to be explicitly defined as such to be beneficial for both parties.

"A mentor is someone who has already achieved what you want to achieve in some way, but with who you can connect on a more personal level as well," claims the former bodybuilder. "You want to picture someone that is kind of like you, but at the next level, if you will. With that in mind, I'd say that a mentor is basically someone who can guide you.

"It's a little hard for me to explain, though, because I've never been the type of guy who has only one mentor. In fact, I don't think I've ever had what you would call 'mentors.' I've had influencers, but I've never really been so transactional in my stuff; meaning that I've never really had a relationship with an influencer where I had to sit down and think about what I could add to that person's life in exchange for their knowledge.

"So, the way I see it, a mentor is someone who's willing to share with you what they know, but in a non-transactional way. In other words, a mentor is someone who's looking for a way to pass on their knowledge to help make the world a better place."

Now, I personally believe that the best relationships—not only when it comes to business, but in life in general—are the ones where value flows both ways and everyone has something to gain from each other.

And although it is true that most mentors typically don't expect to receive as much as they give, I think the best way to keep a healthy mentor-mentee relationship is by making sure both parties involved are continually looking for new ways to provide value to each other.

I bet you would agree with that. In fact, most people would; including Pejman Ghadimi, who was the first to bring up the fact that mentors and coaches are often mistaken.

"To me, a mentor would be a person that you would want to mimic, someone that has reached a higher level of success—a level you aspire to achieve," he said. "A coach, on the other hand, would be someone who's helping you understand the mechanics of a hands-on process—or how to do something step by step, if you will. These are two very different things.

"And because of this lack of differentiation between the two, many people wrongfully believe that mentors are individuals that should be giving you step-by-step instructions on what you should do. If this is what you're looking for, what you need is a coach, not a mentor."

Sharing a similar vision, James Arthur Ray then pushed the concept a little further.

"To answer that question, I think the first thing you need to do is to define the difference between a mentor and a coach," added the *New York Times* bestselling author. "Coaching is a huge industry right now—a $3 billion industry at the time of this conversation. If you walk down the street, everyone and their dog is now a coach.

"And a coach, by and large, is an accountability partner. They're going to ask you what are your goals and tell you what you should do in order to get there. Then, when you get back together a week later, they're going to ask you if you did your homework; you'll say yes or no, and the cycle will start over and over again. That's about it. Of course, I'm oversimplifying here, but you get the idea.

"Coaches teach you tactics; the practical stuff. Michael Jordan had great coaches, and so did Tiger Woods and many others. The problem with tactics is that they rarely—if ever—get applied.

"Mentors, on the other hand, teach principles. From a mentor, you'll learn the big ideas; the philosophies. I'm sure you've heard of the old adage '*Give a man a fish and you'll feed him for a day; teach a man how to fish and you'll feed him for a lifetime.*'

"Well, I believe a real mentor is someone who's going to give you these life principles—which can apply to your health, your business, your finances, and basically everything else in your life—so that you can then figure out the tactics and the strategies on your own.

"For example, imagine you're free rock climbing. A coach is going to be next to you, telling you to put your right foot there and your left hand over there in that crevasse. A mentor is going to be the eagle circling over your head, looking at the broad perspective.

"And because of that; because they've already been in your position and done that before, they can see the snake that's over the next rise. They can see the peak beyond the peak. In other words, a mentor is someone that's going to use their knowledge and their personal experience to offer you a glimpse of the big picture.

"A coach is going to help you with one specific thing, whereas a true mentor is going to have an impact on every single area of your life, teaching you how to access your full potential and inspiration."

And once again, I can't help but think that this is accurate. I mean, based upon my own experience, it is true that real mentorship often goes way beyond the technical aspects of a business or a project.

Take me, for example. When I started working with my first business partner—who eventually became my first mentor as well—all I was looking for was tailored business advice. Yet, I ended up getting a lot more than that.

I learned how to manage my personal finances, how to negotiate and sell, and even how to *think* like a successful entrepreneur.

That's why I believe mentorship is so powerful.

Now, according to Stephanie Nickolich, mentors can sometimes wear different hats, including their coach hat when the circumstances require so.

"To me, a mentor would be defined by somebody who's sharing their successes and failures with you so that you can learn," said the entrepreneur. "It's someone that has your back, someone that's not going to be hired to be your friend, but really to push you to your own limits.

"So, when I hired my first mentor, more specifically—who was really more of a coach at the beginning—I remember feeling extremely uncomfortable every time I would meet with him. In fact, we would meet once a week for several months, and I would cry after every single one of our sessions because he was pushing me to do things that were absolutely out of my comfort zone.

"Looking back, however, I believe that this is exactly what has enabled me to create change and transformation; not only in my business, but in my life as well. So, first and foremost, I would say that a mentor is someone who's capable of pushing you to your own limits.

"But in addition to that, I would say that it's also someone who's willing to share with you their successes and failures, so that you can learn from both of these aspects. Because the truth is, both of these aspects are actually equally important.

"You know, there's a lot of things that I haven't done so well in my business. And now, I can actually teach people how to save time and money as a result of *not* doing some of those things. So, I think that successes are great to help you understand what works, but let's not forget that failures can also be great opportunities for a mentee to learn what *doesn't* work."

Interestingly enough, Stephanie isn't the only one to believe this. Gerard Adams, self-made millionaire by the age of 24, also seems to agree.

"For me, a mentor is somebody that has the ability to inspire you," said the cofounder of *Elite Daily*. "Someone who's in a field you want to learn about. It's someone that can be an advisor to you and teach you based upon their experience—not so much from what they've learned in a book, but from real life experience.

"A mentor is a person that's going to give you tough love. It's someone that's going to tell you what to do, but also what *not* to do. Because I personally believe that a real mentor is someone who has experienced first-hand what not to do, who has learned from it, and who's now there to guide you through your own journey.

"I mean, I myself am a mentor, and I always like to tell people the things that they shouldn't be doing; the things that can save them time and all that stuff. But on the other hand, I also think that a mentor should lead by example. In other words, instead of coaching you based upon their mistakes only, they should also be consistently doing the right things to lead you in the right direction by example, if that makes any sense."

So, if I were to sum it up for you, I would start by saying that a mentor is someone who has personally achieved the kind of results you aspire to achieve yourself. It's a role model, a trusted advisor; someone you can ask for guidance and advice.

Kind of like a private teacher, a mentor is someone who's going to use their experience to help you figure out what to do in a given situation, but also what mistakes to avoid.

Of course, your own definition of mentorship may vary, but this is just to give you an outline of what you should be looking for. Because in order to find what you want, you've got to know what you want. Once you're clear on what it is you desire, that's when all the opportunities will start flowing into your life.

BONUS ANECDOTE WITH DAVE RUEL

If you're familiar with the fitness industry, chances are that you've heard of Dave Ruel—also known as the "Muscle Cook"—since he has been featured in just about every major fitness magazine you can imagine. His golden ticket? The *Anabolic Cooking* cookbook.

And although he has been quite successful over the past few years as an entrepreneur, it wasn't always like that. As a kid, the serial entrepreneur wasn't really good at school. It's only later on that his passion for fitness and bodybuilding led him to come up with his own recipes for healthy and tasty muscle-building meals—which he then decided to sell online.

As a result, ever since he started selling online in 2007, Dave Ruel has made over $16 million in various fields—including publishing, nutrition and personal growth. Today, he spends most of his time traveling the world to make a difference in people's lives and help them grow their own businesses.

And in my opinion, one of the reasons why Dave was able to build such an impressive track record in just a few short years is because he wasn't afraid to reach out to people and ask for advice. As a result, he developed incredible relationships along the way.

"Some of the mentors and influencers that I've invested in early on in my career have now become extremely close friends— pretty much like family," he claims. "Take Vince DelMonte, for example. We've built this great relationship, and now he's promoting my businesses, I'm promoting his, our wives have become really close friends as well, we travel together, have fun together, and all that stuff.

"So, I guess you never know where things are going to lead you when you're looking for influencers like that. And the truth is; we're all humans, so in a way, we're not that different from each others.

"And people often tend to assume that someone is out of reach just because they're out there and they've got a few thousand followers on social media. But that's not true. Especially in this day and age, where you can reach out to pretty much anybody if you're just a little bit connected. It used to be much harder.

"But nowadays, celebrities, singers, experts, mentors; it's never been easier to get in touch with them. So please, never assume that a person is out of reach; just go ahead and try to contact them. You might be surprised!"

If you'd like to learn more about Dave Ruel, visit [http://daveruel.com].

Chapter 2

WHAT ROLE HAVE YOUR MENTORS PLAYED IN YOUR CAREER?

Maybe they're going to help you understand how sales work. Or, on a deeper level, maybe they're going to help you figure out your purpose. Sure enough, I know my mentors have had a tremendous impact on me as an entrepreneur.

So, to help you understand the kind of benefits you can get from having a mentor, I got our six guests to tell me a little more about their own experience.

"I've considered many people as mentors throughout my career—regardless of if it was in Corporate America or in entrepreneurship," started Pejman Ghadimi. "I've always looked up to people who had already done what I wanted to do myself, you know, to understand how they had done it.

"And very soon, I understood that a mentor and a coach were two different things, so I never really looked for individuals who would teach me; instead, I looked for people who would allow me to watch them and learn. There's a huge difference here.

"So, I think this is the role most of my mentors have played in my life; they were always there for me to observe them. Not only that, but in my corporate career, some of them were also able to answer my questions as well—which helped me get a better understanding of the things I had learned from watching their actions.

"And again, this is a big difference between a coach and a mentor. Because while a coach tells you what to do, a mentor doesn't tell you anything," he continued. "Your job is to watch them do what they do and ask your questions as they arise. Only then it becomes the mentor's responsibility to provide you with some answers.

"You know, anyone can be a mentor to anyone. They don't even have to physically have that title. And I think one of the reasons why most people are having a hard time finding mentors is because they go to someone and ask to be mentored when by definition, what they're really looking for is coaching.

"If you're looking for weekly meetings, discussions, or step by step instructions to understand what a person has done and how they've done it; then you're looking for coaching. When you think of mentorship, on the other hand, it all comes down to *you* as an individual.

"I mean, you could even have the president of the United States as a mentor. You could look up to what he's doing and try to analyze and understand his behavior. Now, for obvious reasons, interaction would be very difficult with a president, so I guess that would be a downside.

"But let's say you find a local business owner that you can observe and learn from. Well, the fact that he's allowing you to ask questions and that he's providing you with some answers, that alone would be enough to make him a mentor—even if there isn't any specific agenda in place."

One thing's for sure; this is probably one the most effective ways to learn. I mean, coaches are great to point you in the right direction and give you clear instructions. But at the end of the day, I think the only way to really get to understand a concept is by seeing it from your own perspective—not from your coach's perspective.

"You know, I'm a big believer in this idea that everyone should be working on building their own style," added Dave Ruel. "Most people think that in order to be successful, you need to find a mentor and try to do the exact same things that they've done.

"Well, I think that's a huge mistake. Instead, what you should really focus on is finding a mentor who can influence and guide you, of course, but who can also inspire you to create your own style and see things from your own perspective.

"I'm a big fan of the mentors you can come up to and ask for some guidance with the big questions—like when you have an important decision to make or a bold business move you want to talk about.

"That's why I love masterminds. Because in a mastermind, you take advice from people, but at the same time, you always have to stay true to yourself and try to come up with a way of your own, which I think is pretty cool."

So, I guess an important lesson you could draw from these lines is the fact that, first and foremost, mentors are human like you and I. And thus, their way of doing things doesn't have to be the only way. In fact, the best mentors usually are the ones who inspire you to use their advice as a starting point rather than as an absolute truth.

The point being that you can definitely use it as an opportunity to learn and grow— I'd be the first to encourage you to do so— but always make sure you stay true to yourself along the way. Like John Mason said, *'You were born an original, don't die a copy.'*

Now, for his part, James Arthur Ray claims that his mentors have helped him find what he likes to call his own "inner genius."

"My mentors have played a massive role in my life—not only in my career, but in my life in general as well," he admitted. "In fact, they were all what I defined earlier as true mentors; none of them were coaches. So, they were able to help me connect with my inspiration, if you will.

"You know, I've built a $10 million company using nothing more than a vision, a few credit cards and a tremendous work ethic. And it wasn't always easy, but deep down inside, I knew all of these sacrifices and efforts would eventually pay off; I knew I was at the right place.

"And I think that when you know exactly 'why' you're here, when you're on point and on purpose; that's when work doesn't feel like work anymore. It just becomes something else; you work hard, but it's hardly work.

"As a result, you'll work for days, months and even years, but it won't feel like what you would normally call 'work.' That's something my mentors have helped me understand.

"So, I would say that most of my mentors have been in the camp of providing me with these overarching principles. The ones that have allowed me to connect with my inspiration and find guidance when I needed it the most. And I feel like that's the greatest gift that they ever gave me; to not reveal me their own truth, but to help me unveil my own."

In other words, you want to build a solid foundation for your success. You want to work on your character as an individual; on what makes you who you are. And to some people, that's what mentors are for; to help you deal with these things.

Now, from what he told me, Gerard Adams also seems to agree with James on that.

"I've had multiple mentors throughout my life, and even to this day I continue to seek for new mentors," said Gerard. "It's pretty simple; I think you should always be looking for new ways to surround yourself with people that have more wisdom and more experience than you. Because as the saying goes; if you're the smartest person in the room, then you're in the wrong room.

"That being said, the first mentors I had were both my mother and my father. And I remember when I was younger, my father would always leave these little notes for me in different places of the house. For example, he knew that I would open up the fridge in the morning, so he would leave a note in there; some quote of a president or a famous Roman emperor. He just did that all the time. So, my father instilled leadership in me at a very young age.

"My mother, on the other hand, taught me how to love, how to not take things for granted and how to develop a very good work ethic. From her, I learned that I was unique as a person; that money might come and go, but that no one can take away from you what forms your character as an individual.

"And so, she taught me that even if you lose the shirt off your back, you can always go back and rebuild what you've lost, as long as you know who you are as person. Because at a point in her life, she did lose everything; my grandparents had a fire and they ended up losing literally everything they had. So, I would say that both my mother and my father had a very positive impact on me as my first mentors."

While it is true that a mentor can sometimes help you deal with your emotions and figure out who you are as an individual, for others, like Stephanie Nickolich, it's what I would define more as the 'surface' work that has really made the biggest difference.

"Along with the various coaches that I've worked with," started the entrepreneur, "I'd say that my mentors have played a very significant role in my career. So, I truly believe in the importance of having a mentor in your journey; I think it's important to have somebody that you can just bounce ideas off of every once in a while.

"Because sometimes, especially us as creative entrepreneurs, we have all these crazy ideas that we want to turn into reality. So, it becomes very important to stay on track and make sure that the things we do are serving the bigger vision we have for our success. And since we're so close to our day-to-day operations, sometimes it's really hard to see the problems that exist in our own business.

"So, for those reasons, I would say that 100% of the reason why I am where I am today is because I've had the support, the guidance and the accountability of my mentors, along with a swift kick in the butt when necessary. That's what really made the biggest difference for me."

It's pretty hard to disagree. I mean, while Gerard and James are certainly right on the fact that mentorship can help you on a much deeper level, I also think that Stephanie has a point here. Without falling into coaching, I think it's also part of a mentor's role to provide you with their support and guidance for the things that are happening in your life on a smaller scale.

"You know, every step along the way, no matter where I was in my career, I've always had people to look up to and get advice from," added Doug Sandler. "And in my opinion, that can only be a good thing.

"Now, when I'm looking for a mentor, I always try to pick someone who's just a few years ahead of me—maybe not agewise, but a few years ahead of me in terms of where I am in my career, for example. I always try to figure out the things I want to achieve first, and then I focus on how I want to get there.

"So, whenever I'm looking for advice, I try to find the people who can potentially help me, and then I ask them for specific instructions on what that they think I should do differently. Because for me, it's all about guidance and accountability. I think accountability is very important when it comes to mentorship.

"So, in every single phase of my career, I've had people like that—whether you want to call them mentors, coaches, or advisers— to help me get going and stay on the right path. And the truth is; we don't live in a vacuum. We live in this world where there are plenty of people who know much more than we do about all sorts of things. So, why try to reinvent the wheel when another guy has already invented it? Instead, why not just ask him for advice and see where this is going to lead you? If someone has already been down that road before, they probably know a thing or two that are going to help you."

All things considered, everyone seems to agree on the fact that mentors can have a pretty significant impact on you as a person. Whether it's by helping you figure out who you are as an individual, what makes your character so unique, or by providing you with their support and guidance, it's clear that mentors can definitely help you get going in the right direction.

BONUS ANECDOTE WITH DOUG SANDLER

With over 30 years of business experience as an entrepreneur, a business owner, a manager and a staff member, Doug Sandler is the author of *Nice Guys Finish First*, which came out in 2015 and quickly became a #1 ranked Amazon bestseller.

His expertise revolves around making connections, building relationships and strengthening bonds both inside and outside organizations. However, don't let the "Mr. Nice Guy" tag mislead you, as Doug has entered into many high level negotiations and is known to be anything but a pushover.

The speaking and consulting business he has built over the past few years is geared towards both improving relationships and winning business through his time-tested sales, service and relationship building system. So, not only is Doug Sandler a nationally recognized speaker, but his podcast,

The Nice Guys on Business, is also one of the top business podcasts out there.

As a result, Doug has been titled by a leading social media marketing company as one of the top 100 Social Media Influencers to follow.

And according to the man himself, it would've been much harder to get to this point without the help and the guidance of a few mentors along the way.

"When I first started to get into the speaking business, as well as when I first started to write my book, all of this was still pretty new to me," he said. "And honestly, I don't know if I would've been able to make it this far without the help of a coach or a mentor, simply because there was no other way for me to know for sure if I was doing the right thing or not when I was first starting out.

"You know, if you think about it, writing a book is just putting words on paper. However, I can tell you for a fact that you never know what questions you're going to have until you actually start writing those words; you just never know until they come up.

"So, I guess if there is any shortcut to success, it would be to listen to what other people have already done before you, and then to apply the advice they give you. It doesn't mean that you'll achieve success in the same way they did, but it sure will give you a benchmark to refer to. Just follow what they've done, follow the instructions, and maybe you'll be able to achieve what they achieved in your own way."

If you'd like to learn more about Doug Sandler and his book, *Nice Guys Finish First*, feel free to check out his website at [http://dougsandler.com].

Chapter 3

WHAT IS THE BEST ADVICE THAT YOU'VE EVER GOTTEN FROM ONE OF YOUR MENTORS?

So far, we've seen that mentors can sometimes wear a lot of different hats, going anywhere from being your trusted advisors to helping you out with a very specific business matter. That's just another proof of how beneficial a great mentor-mentee relationship can be.

Speaking for myself, I would even say that the most important life lessons I've learned came directly from my mentors. Therefore, when I asked the six entrepreneurs for the Holy Grail of all the advice that they had ever gotten, my expectations were quite high.

But one thing's for sure; once you read those lines and you actually apply the advice that's in there, chances are that your perspective will be changed forever. Because the truth is; these lessons really do have the power to change your life.

Here's exactly what I'm talking about:

"As I was coming to my maturity as a businessman, my next mentor taught me a lot about failure," started Gerard Adams. "And I feel like that's why my definition of mentorship is a lot about understanding what *not* to do just as much—if not more—as what to do.

"So, my first business mentor taught me about an entire industry. He taught me some tactics that had worked for him, so that I could analyze them and implement them into my life. Now, what's interesting is that, as I was working for him as a mentee—I was doing marketing for him at the time—I got to learn from his mistakes in real time.

"And I remember, one day he asked me to set up this big demonstration to raise money for one of our products. So, I rented a venue, got a stage, found a couple of TVs to showcase the product. I did the invitation list, checked people in, did a speech in front of everybody, introduced him, and even managed to get a few potential investors and media people in the room.

"But then, when the chief scientist officer came up front to show the product and prove it, he hit the button... And it didn't work. Everything went to shit. In a moment's time, the guy could've raised tens of millions of dollars, but by making a silly mistake—by not preparing correctly—he immediately lost the opportunity of a lifetime.

"On top of that, the company was publicly traded; so when the news came out, all the stocks went down significantly. So, as much as I feel like this mentor has helped me become the entrepreneur that I am today by teaching me all those tactics and strategies, I feel like watching him fail for not having prepared correctly was probably one of the greatest lessons I've ever learned."

Just like that, he could've scored one of the best home runs of his career, but instead, he let a simple lack of preparation take away this huge opportunity. That's a very powerful lesson.

And don't get me wrong; I'm not saying that you should spend your days planning everything and never stop until it's perfect. There's a time for planning, yes, but there's also a time for execution. When you find the right balance between the two, that's when you'll start winning.

On the other hand, when I asked Stephanie Nickolich the same question, her answer went as follows.

"I feel like, throughout my life, my parents have really encouraged me to believe that I could achieve anything I wanted to. And to be honest, I think this holds a very important role in how I've developed and evolved as a person, but also as a business owner and as a mom, because I truly believe that anything is possible once you put your mind to it.

"So, I think it's important to have someone on your team that believes in your mission and your vision just as much as you do—if not more than you do. I say that because I'm a huge thinker; I get these gigantic visions, and I would never want someone to tell me that my ideas aren't good enough.

"At the end of the day, you've got to trust that absolutely anything is possible—I'm truly convinced of that. And therefore, I would say that if your dreams don't scare you, they're probably not big enough."

In the same vein, Pejman Ghadimi claims that just because your day job doesn't allow you to buy your dream house, for example, it doesn't mean that there's no other way for you to get what you want. Because if you want it bad enough, you will find a way to make it happen.

"Unfortunately, I don't have a cheesy quote to give you," said the self-made millionaire. "But I think one of the biggest things I've learned was during my banking career. I had an amazing mentor at that time, a good friend of mine. And what he showed me is that just because you work at a certain job, or just because you have a certain passion—no matter what it is—it doesn't have to dictate your whole life.

"What I mean is that although we were in banking and we were making good money, it was certainly not enough to be driving around in a Ferrari or a Lamborghini. However, this man showed me that if you really want those things, like the fancy cars and the nice watches, you can have them by doing other stuff, like having a business on the side. You know, there's a million ways you can get what you want aside from working at your day job.

"For example, look at the teachers out there—there's a lot of teachers in the educational system who complain about the fact that they don't make enough money. Well, the fact that you don't make enough money being a teacher doesn't mean that you can't do anything else aside from teaching to get to the financial status that you want. That's something I've learned pretty quickly during my corporate career.

"So, to answer your question; the best piece of advice that I've ever gotten would be to never let your environment dictate the level of success you're going to achieve."

This makes a lot of sense, especially since you don't have to be particularly creative to come up with an idea nowadays. All you need is a good marketing strategy to support your idea and connect the dots between your offer and your buyers, and that's it.

Creating a business has never been easier. We have the privilege to live in an era where the entire world is just a few clicks away from us. And from a marketing standpoint, that means you can literally monetize anything.

All you have to do is to take the leap of faith and never look back—which brings me to Doug Sandler's point: don't be afraid to fail.

"I think the best piece of advice I've ever gotten goes way back to when I first got into the business world," affirmed Doug. "It was from my dad, and he said: 'Don't be afraid to fail.'

"But what it meant to me was really just: 'Don't give up.' Because whatever you do, you've got to understand that achieving success is something that doesn't happen overnight. You'll face a lot of obstacles along the way, and I can promise you that it's not going to be a straight line.

"In fact, if you look back at your career, chances are that you'll see a lot of zigzags, decisions and crossing roads. And as long as you stay focused on your destination, I think none of these choices can be wrong. You just need to make sure that you keep moving forward after making that decision, and that you keep your head high no matter what. But never let failure—or the fear of failure—hold you back from taking action."

Interestingly enough, Dave Ruel seems to agree. And like Pejman Ghadimi, he also claims that you should never let your fears or your direct environment dictate the level of success you achieve. Here's what he had to say about that:

"The truth is; I've received so much great advice that I wouldn't be able to tell," confessed Dave. "I know it's not the kind of answer you expected, but that's just not how I think; I never think of only one specific answer. Instead, what I like to do is to pick one little thing here, another little piece there, and then build my own vision from that. And in a certain way, I think this mindset is probably one of the reasons why I am where I am today.

"Now, with that being said, here's my motto; figure it out and get shit done. In other words, I think everything in life can be figured out—especially in this day and age, where you're just a few clicks away from literally any specific answer you could be looking for.

"With that in mind, I would say that one of the most important things I've learned from my influencers is that you've got to be resourceful; you've got to be able to figure things out. If you don't know how to do something, then hire someone to do it for you. But never be limited by the things you don't know.

"Because like Gary Vaynerchuk says, most of today's problems have already been thought about. And the reason why they still exist is because 99% of people never take action on their ideas.

"Now, when you put things in motion, you usually get a result—whatever it is. But if you don't do anything, nothing's going to happen. So, whenever you get an idea, just figure out what you need to know and then take immediate action on it. That's how you'll generate results."

In fact, by applying this simple—yet wildly underrated—principle, not only will you generate results, but that's also how you'll keep evolving as a person. And if you've ever been stuck in a project or something, you know how important this is.

Which brings me to James Arthur Ray's best advice: "Never get comfortable, and always go bold." In other words, you can either be the guy who finishes the marathon, or the one who wins the marathon. We'll talk a little more about what this means in James' bonus anecdote, but as of right now, I think it gives you a pretty good idea of what you can expect from a good mentor.

But at the end of the day, although it is true that a mentor can help and guide you, it's still up to you to decide whether or not you're going to apply the advice you get. Because knowledge isn't going to help you if you never implement it. That's something these entrepreneurs were quick to understand, and I think it's part of the reason why they all became so successful.

BONUS ANECDOTE WITH JAMES ARTHUR RAY

James Arthur Ray is a *New York Times* bestselling author who is also known for his success in the business world. In fact, his former company was featured on the *Inc.*

500 list in 2009 as one of the fastest grow-ing privately held companies in the United States.

But after rising to the top of his industry, the man literally lost everything he had in the same year—from the business that took him 20 years to build to his entire life sav-ings, his home, his reputation and ultimate-ly, his liberty.

Today, however, the man claims that the experience of losing everything has actually allowed him to realize quite a few things, including the fact that anyone can turn their entire life around by learning how to make adversity an ally.

James is also one of the coauthors of *The Secret*, a feature-length film and *New York Times* bestseller on its own, and has been featured many times on national TV shows, like *The Oprah Winfrey Show*, *Good Morn-ing America*, *The Today Show*, *Piers Mor-gan Live* and *CNN's Larry King Live*.

"You know, back in the late 1990s, I was in the personal performance industry, and I was still fairly new in this field," said James. "And at first, I was teaching a lot of skills—sales strategies, team building and leadership tips, etc. But soon, it got very frustrating for me, because I realized that all these skills just wouldn't be applied.

"So, after conducting some research, what I recognized is that your psychology always drives your strategy. In other words, the way that you think and feel is always going to determine how you act. And since I really wanted to be able to create a profound shift in people's results, I had to start dealing with the cause, not the effect.

"Long story short, I told my mentor at the time that I wanted to write a book about it. And straight up, he told me that there was no money to be made with a book—you know, real appreciable money—that instead, what you get from a book is reach. For that reason, he told me that I had to come up with a program—remember, we were in the '90s, so we're talking about an audio cassette program here.

"So, I put this together and I was very proud of it; I now had my first program. And to get there, I really had to go bold and take a lot of risks, because the production costs were huge and I didn't have the money at the time. But right from the start, the man was encouraging me to play big and go bold.

"And what I've learned is that when you take the leap of faith and just go all-in, that's when the Universe seems to look down on you and give you all the support you need. I know that sounds completely illogical, but that's how my top performing clients think and act... And guess what; it works.

"So, I called my mentor to let him know that I had just received the first cassettes, and all he said was: 'Alright. What are you going to do next?' Not exactly the kind of reaction I expected.

"I mean, I had just opened the box and he was already asking for the next thing. I didn't understand... But then he added: 'What are you going to do? Rest on your laurels?' And I knew he was right; I had to keep building momentum. So, I got back to work and created my next program; and then my first book, and that's when things really began to spin off for me.

"Because if something is worth doing, it's worth doing big. I truly believe this. So, make bold moves, and never get comfortable. That's the best advice I've ever gotten."

To learn more about James Arthur Ray and download his free guide to find your purpose and turn your life around, visit his website at [http://jamesray.com/living-on-purpose-survey].

Chapter 4

HOW DO YOU THINK A MENTOR CAN HELP YOU FULFILL YOUR DREAMS?

Going through the next chapter, you'll notice that this is probably the one where opinions vary the most from one another. Some people will say that mentors will show you the way and save you a lot of time; others will claim that mentors just won't do the work for you.

I like to think that I stand kind of in the middle. I mean, it is true that a mentor is definitely not going to do the work for you—like I've said before, you've got to be willing to put in the efforts yourself. However, I do believe that a mentor can make it easier for

you to get where you want to be. And that's
what I wanted to clarify with this chapter.

"A mentor can definitely save you a lot of
time," said Dave Ruel right off the bat. "But
I don't think a mentor can make you succeed. At the end of the day, I think you're
the only one who can make yourself succeed.

"You know, a mentor is usually someone
you can look up to; someone who has 'been
there and done that.' As a result, they probably know things that you don't know yet.
And it's good to have people like this in your
life. You can call them mentors; I like to call
them influencers.

"But ultimately, you're responsible for
your own success; you're the one who's
going to put in the work. Your mentor isn't
going to make it happen for you. Besides, a
mentor is never going to invest in someone
who can't get shit done. They want hustlers;
they want people who have the ability to
keep moving forward even when the problems start to arise.

"So, the way I see it, the only thing a
mentor can do to help you fulfill your
dreams is to point you in the right direction

when you need it, using what they know as a starting point. And I think that alone should be enough to save you a lot of time."

Similarly, here's what Doug Sandler then told me:

"You know, when I provide advice, I can usually do it in two different ways. I can provide it in theory, which is basically me sharing a thought or an inspiration, or I can provide it in practical steps—which would be more like following a recipe.

"So, I think a mentor is someone who can provide you with a big picture view. They can help you envision the final result you want, and then break it down into smaller steps that you can take to get there. And believe me when I say this; I'm a big picture guy, but sometimes, it feels good to see things from a different angle and follow the smaller steps.

"For example, if someone asked me how to get 20,000 engaged followers on Twitter, I would probably start by telling them that they need to share great content. But then, I would go a little deeper in the strategies and tell them that I've used a certain software, blogged that many times a week, etc. And I think that's how a mentor can help you fulfill your dreams; by providing you with that kind of support and guidance."

It's hard for me to argue with that. I think mentors can definitely help you see things from a different angle, especially when it comes to your dreams or your goals. And although at first it may sound like he doesn't agree at all, Pejman Ghadimi actually came up with a very interesting answer to complement Doug's point of view.

According to him, mentors also have the ability to create the image of a possibility in your mind—not to dictate how far you can go, but rather to open your eyes to the world of possibilities that's in front of you.

"The truth is, nobody can help you fulfill your dreams other than yourself," said the founder of *Secret Entourage* during the interview. "What a mentor *can* do, however, is to help you develop a better understanding of what's possible for you.

"For example, let's say you're running in the Olympics and you've seen someone run the track in three minutes—which had never been done before. Well, that's going to be the new baseline you'll use for comparing yourself. Therefore, if it takes you five minutes to do the same thing, chances are that you'll be disappointed. But it's not said anywhere that you can't do it in under three minutes and break the world record.

"What I'm trying to say is that having someone who's already been down the same path and has already achieved a certain result doesn't dictate how far you'll go—it's nothing more than a baseline for you to understand where things fit. In other words, it basically gives you perspective on things that you don't necessarily understand.

"And because we, as human beings, understand measurement—we like to measure how good we are, how much money we have, how far we've come—that baseline enables us to measure where we stand.

"So, like we've talked earlier; if most teachers make $40k a year and you know you're making $50k, then you won't complain, because you know you're making way more than the average teacher. But if you go ahead and become a teacher thinking that they're making $200k, and someone tells you that the salary is actually $35k, you'll feel like something is wrong. That's why you need to have a baseline.

"When you have a mentor to help you understand all of this, that's when your expectations usually become aligned with your beliefs. And as a result, that's when your goals and your dreams ultimately become very real and measurable."

In the same vein, James Arthur Ray also made it very clear that it's up to each and everyone of us to take responsibility for our own success.

"Of course, the mentor can't do it for you," added the bestselling author. "Every single one of us has to climb their own mountain. Every top performer in any given field had to get there on their own; no one was dropped on the top of the mountain by helicopter.

"What a mentor can do, though, is to cut your learning curve in half. So, my advice would be the following; you have to have a mentor. Plato had Socrates, Aristotle had Plato, and Alexander the Great had Aristotle; you've got to have one. With their advice and their principles, I think mentors can definitely help you accelerate your journey to success. And that, my friend, is worth its weight in gold."

I couldn't agree more. I mean, sure, you can always learn from your own mistakes, but the truth is; it can sometimes be a pretty expansive way to learn.

That's why I think finding a mentor who's already been there before is probably the best thing you can do when starting something new. It's going to save you a lot of time and money, but most importantly— to me, anyway—it's going to save you a lot of headaches.

And when I asked Stephanie Nickolich for her thoughts on the subject, she seemed to share the same opinion.

"I think it all starts with you being one hundred percent committed to doing the work," said the entrepreneur. "Because you don't hire a mentor, a coach or a consultant if you're not a hundred percent committed to taking action—otherwise, you're just going to waste your money.

"But if you're willing to show up, get un-comfortable, get vulnerable and play full out; then I think a mentor can absolutely help you fulfill your dreams. Whether it's through their own personal experiences, their education or their professional background; mentors can definitely help you get the results you want. But again, you've got to be willing to commit yourself."

So, just like Dave and I, Stephanie seems to agree on the fact that ultimately, the best way that a mentor can help you get what you want is by using their experience—aka the lessons that they've learned through their successes and failures—to guide you through your own journey.

And that's what I love about mentorship; the fact that you get to benefit from someone else's experience in your own journey to success. If you think about it, that's huge!

"I always say that mentorship is probably the most invaluable asset that you can have in your life to help you succeed," added Gerard Adams in response to my initial question. "But at the end of the day, I feel like there's not that much a mentor can do aside from guiding you in the right direction. Because you know the saying; you can only lead a horse to water, but you can't make it drink.

"So, the best thing a mentor can do is to show you their path; what worked for them and what didn't work. They can offer you the experience and the wisdom that they have, the mistakes that they've made and the mindset that you need to have, but at the end of the day, it is your job as the mentee to really implement that knowledge into your life and to hold yourself accountable for it. Because once again, a mentor isn't going to do the work for you."

Now, if there's only one thing you should understand from this chapter—or this entire book, for that matter—it's the latter. I just cannot stress this enough; a mentor isn't going to do the work for you. A mentor is someone who's going to give you a roadmap and help you figure out the things you should focus on.

In short, whether it's by providing you with a different perspective on what it is you're trying to accomplish or by shaving time out of your learning curve, I think we all agree on the fact that a mentor can definitely help you fulfill your dreams. As a mentee, on the other hand, your job is to take responsibility for your own success and make things happen.

Once you get a grasp of this very simple concept, that's when you'll start seeing the results in your life.

BONUS ANECDOTE WITH STEPHANIE NICKOLICH

Stephanie Nickolich—also know as the "Millionista Mentor"—is a thriving entrepreneur known for helping other women crush their doubts, master what she calls their "money mindset" and capitalize on their strengths to skyrocket their success.

After making heads turn for the first time as a sales strategist in the corporate world, where she helped building a $1.2 million company in just a year's time, Stephanie left her job to create the e-commerce empire *Accessory Fanatic*, where she ended up getting her first real taste of entrepreneurial success.

Looking for a way to make a positive impact in the world, she then created *Success Society*, an online community where women in business can connect, collaborate and capitalize on their dreams. As a result, Stephanie now uses her fun and outspoken approach to inspire, empower and educate businesswomen worldwide—but most importantly, she's doing what she loves!

"You know, the internet being what it is, most of my revenue is now generated directly through *Facebook Ads*," said Stephanie. "And I know that every time I spend $1,000 on them, I typically make around $10,000. So, let's just say that I spend a hell of a lot of money on there.

"However, when I first started playing around with *Facebook Ads*, I had these big goals and big ambitions, so I hired somebody to help me out with them. I ended up spending $13,000 on the ads themselves, plus $10,000 in service fees. Yet, I made a grand total of only $8,000 out of that campaign... Now, if you do the math, that was a pretty horrible experience.

"But from that experience, I learned that as a business owner, I would need to know enough about my business to be able to make informed decisions about it. And because of that, not only am I in a position where I can now help people avoid going down the same path, but I can also help them right out of the gate to set up the right strategy behind their ads, so that they can achieve their goals.

"So yes, a mentor can definitely save you a lot of time and money, but beyond that, I think a mentor can also *make* you a lot of money.

"That being said, let me ask you this; if you knew that paying somebody thousands of dollars today could make you a hundred times that in the near future—simply because they have the knowledge, the education and the experience to take you from where you are to where you want to be—wouldn't it be worth spending the money to hire that person? If you ask me, the answer is absolutely! You've got to focus on the value.

"And here's two things that people value most; time and money. So, if I can save someone money—not even make them money, but just save them tens of thousands of dollars—and cover the costs of my services, so that they can leave educated about how to run their business and create more success, then I think it's worth the investment. The same goes with time; if I can shave time out of their learning curve by helping them avoid a bunch of mistakes, it's totally worth it.

"Of course, if you want to go and figure this out by yourself, go ahead! I mean, it's going to cost you thousands of dollars more, and it's probably going to take you three years to do what you could've done in six months, but you can do it if that's what you want. Again, you need to focus on the value.

"So, when I first started working with my mentor, I was looking for two things; the mindset and the money game that I hoped to achieve. I picked the person that I thought could help me out with both, and it's been a great fit ever since.

"Now, to be honest with you, I do not run my own *Facebook Ads* today, but I am heavily involved in the strategy behind the ads themselves. In addition, I'm also very clear with my team about what our numbers are on a regular basis. And so far, it's working pretty well!"

To learn more about Stephanie Nickolich and what she's up to, you can visit her website at [http://stephanienickolich.com].

Chapter 5

WHAT WOULD BE YOUR ADVICE TO SOMEONE LOOKING FOR A MENTOR?

Let's face it; finding a mentor can sometimes be a pretty hefty task, especially when you have no idea where to start. And if you're reading this book right now, my guess is that you know exactly what I'm talking about.

That's one of the reasons why I love this chapter so much; because of all the practical steps and advice it contains. In fact, all the tips you'll find in there actually come from people who have personally been on both sides of the fence.

In other words, not only have they been through the process of *getting* a mentor, but they also know what it's like to *be* a mentor—which I think brings a very interesting perspective and a lot of additional value to their answers.

So, without any further ado, let's dive in and see what kind of advice our six guests have to share with us, starting with Gerard Adams.

"First and foremost, I think you need to figure out what it is that you're interested in; what it is that you're passionate about. That's going to help you pinpoint who are the people that you can relate to.

"And then, once you understand what it is that drives you, I think you should start studying the marketplace. You want someone who's got a story that you can relate to, but also someone who has a certain expertise in their field.

"Now, you've probably heard a lot of people talking about this before, but as a mentee, you can't just expect the relationship to be a one-way street. It's a two-way street, where both sides have to provide value.

"One way of making this work would be to create something. Use what you know to create something that's going to prove the mentor that you can actually bring value to the table—in other words, give them a good reason to invest in you.

"Besides, I think it's also a matter of persistence. And I'm not talking about sending them an email every single day—that's never going to work. But maybe there's something creative that you can send them. Or maybe you can attend to one of their speaking engagements and get a few minutes to start building a relationship with them. Be creative.

"As a matter of fact, I think the more you can do to actually get in front of these people and show them your worth, the better. You know, I get a lot of requests on a daily basis from people who want me to mentor them. But at the end of the day, very few of them actually manage to catch my attention in some way.

"For instance, I've had someone using their connections to help me get featured in various magazines, someone introducing me to another person, etc. Now, these are just examples, but you get the idea; if you want to get noticed, you need to bring value.

"And sometimes, well, I guess you just have to buy a one-way ticket, fly, and figure out a way to make it happen once you get there. I mean, I've had mentees who really wanted to meet me do just that. They bought a one-way ticket to New York, flew in without even telling me, and then they figured out a way to meet me on the spot. They got in front of me and showed me that they were very serious. That's it. They didn't care about what they had to do; they just did it."

Unfortunately, we tend to forget how powerful a simple commitment like this can be. But what it shows is that you're willing to take risks. And for someone who's contemplating the possibility of mentoring you, this can be a very decisive factor—because once again, mentors are not going to invest in someone who can't get things done.

So, my advice would be the following: whenever you're facing a situation like this, just ask yourself if the potential return is worth taking the risk. And then, act accordingly.

Because on a certain level, buying a one-way ticket to New York without even knowing if the person you want to meet is going to be in town can be pretty risky—especially if you don't have the money. But if everything does work out, you could end up having a mentor to help you make your dreams come true—which is worth a lot more than just a few hundred bucks, if you ask me. So, I guess sometimes you just have to take the risk.

Now, according to Doug Sandler, your best bet would be to find a mentor that's just a few years ahead of you in terms of where you want to be. Here's why:

"I would probably look at someone in my field or in my industry who has already developed the kind of relationships that I'd like to have," he said. "Also, I would make sure to pick someone who has already achieved the kind of results that I want.

"However, I would be careful not to put that mentor too far out there. Meaning that if I wanted to be a movie star, I don't think that the first person I'd look at would be someone who has been around for 40 years and has already achieved everything there is to achieve in the industry.

"Instead, I would probably start talking to people that are just a few years ahead of me. And the reason why is very simple. I feel like sometimes, the people who have achieved such a high level of success might have forgotten what it was like at the beginning. Or else, things may simply have changed in the meantime—especially with today's technology.

"So yeah, that would be my advice to someone looking for a mentor."

On a different note, Stephanie Nickolich also made it very clear that one of the first things you should be looking for in a mentor is their ability to help you improve your mindset.

"For starters, I would absolutely look for someone who is in alignment with the mindset that I want," added Stephanie. "See, that's the number one reason why I was never able to achieve the level of success that I wanted to achieve; because my mindset was all screwed up. I wasn't trained to think like a successful CEO. In fact, I was so focused on my current reality and my problems that I couldn't even see two feet in front of them.

"So, when I met my mentor, I noticed that his mindset was very different. Actually, I could tell that from our very first conversation, where I remember thinking: 'What a sharp guy; he really knows what's up!'

"And that was very attractive to me as a mentee, because it showed me that he thought very differently—which is exactly what I needed for my business. So, that would be the first thing on the list; I would seek for someone who has the mindset that I want."

Although this is clearly a step in the right direction, Pejman Ghadimi, for his part, wanted to highlight the importance of approaching people from the right angle.

"I'll give you the advice that I give to everyone who thinks that somehow, they absolutely need a mentor to be successful," he said. "You don't need a mentor to be successful; you need a mentor to believe. That's it. That's the only thing you need a mentor for.

"So, with that in mind, here's what I would suggest you to do; don't approach people asking them for a formalized mentor plan. And most importantly, don't approach them because of the things that they have acquired—like the cars and the watches. These are the two most common mistakes that people make when seeking for a mentor.

"Instead, you want to approach them in a way that shows that you actually understand what they've done, not just what they have acquired. Which means, if the person in front of you has opened the largest car dealership in the world, and has enjoyed selling 800 cars a month while every other dealership was selling 500, then maybe your conversation shouldn't be based upon them driving a Ferrari. Instead, maybe it should be based upon you trying to figure out what they've done to make their dealership so successful.

"The point being: mentors will take interest in people who care about what they do, not about what they have. You know, so many people come to me saying: 'Can you mentor me? I want to be successful like you.' But most of the time, my answer to them is very simple: 'No.' Because I hate that approach.

"But if someone comes to me with a specific question, saying: 'I've read your book, I get what you're saying when you're talking about awareness, but how do you apply the principles you mentioned on page 19?' I'm going to get out of my way and write them a long paragraph. I might even get on the phone with them. But I'm going to answer them in some way, because they made an effort, and I want them to understand the principles I teach.

"So, it's a lot more appealing for mentors to say yes and help out you when you can show that you've actually done your research.

"Unfortunately, though, when people are looking for mentors, they're always focused on the reward, and never on the work. But the truth is; when you conduct your research, and then contact the person and say: 'I've watched a dozen of your interviews, I've read your book, and I still have a question...' then you allow the conversation to take a whole new direction. And that's how you get people to listen to you."

In other words, you need to do your homework and show that you actually care about the person's accomplishments. Because obviously, if you don't genuinely care, then you shouldn't be asking them for advice in the first place.

Now, we've talked about how value should be flowing both ways between both the mentor and the mentee earlier in this chapter. But Dave Ruel really took this idea up a notch by implying that you should also invest in your mentor's programs and masterminds if you have a chance.

"Overall, I think one of the most effective strategies to get someone to be your mentor would be to offer them massive value," added the self-made millionaire. "That's how you'll get noticed.

"Another way would be to make the commitment and the investment to get physically there and meet them in person. So, invest in their masterminds if you can, go to their events, invest in their programs; just prove them in some way that you're serious and that you're worth their time.

"Because a mentor isn't going to invest in someone who has no chance of making it; they're going to go with the odds and stick to the people who they think can get things done and really make a difference. That's why you need to be smart and show them that you're valuable."

And make no mistake; this isn't just about money. It's about showing that you care enough to make the commitment and to invest in yourself. And judging by his answer, James Arthur Ray seems to agree with Dave and I on that.

"You need to invest in your growth," said James. "It's part of the process. You know, I have personally invested incredible amounts of time and money in mentorship. For example; a few years back, when I was living in San Diego, I had a mentor in Toronto. And one day, he asked me to fly there and go spend the weekend hanging out with him. Now, I didn't have the money at that time, but I knew one thing; I couldn't afford *not* to do it.

"So, I borrowed money from my parents, jumped on a plane, and it turned out to be one of the most pivotal points of my entire life. The point being; you've got to be willing to do whatever it takes to spend time with your mentors and study with them. You've got to focus on the value.

"You know, Mark Cuban doesn't pay his apprentices, and he gets a lot of negative press for that. But the truth is that his people actually get a lot of value out of this experience—way more value than the money they could've made during that time.

"So, sometimes you've got to be able to humble yourself and look at the bigger picture. For instance, I remember flying to Hawaii at some point—and I was already making multiple millions of dollars at that time—but I ended up volunteering there for two weeks, just to be a part of this event my mentor was hosting.

"And the truth is: I could've made a lot of money during that time. But I knew that being there with my mentor was a lot more valuable. So, what I'm saying is that it won't necessarily be fun all the time, but on the long run, it's definitely going to be worth it.

"You might also want to choose a mentor who has been there and done that. Because you know, nowadays, everybody and their dog claims to be a coach. I mean, all you have to do is to take a course, build your website, and boom; you're good to go. Well, not so fast! You want to choose a mentor who has already been where you want to be and done what you want to do.

"For example; if I wanted to learn about real estate, then I would call Donald Trump, because he sure knows what he's talking about when it comes to real estate. If I wanted to learn about internet technologies, I would talk to Mark Cuban. And if I wanted to talk about creativity and innovation, then I would have a chat with Richard Branson. You get the point.

"Now, before you get going with all these strategies, one thing I would recommend is that you find your 'inner genius.' In other words, you need to find what it is that you're gifted with, and then you need to start developing that gift. Because from the time we were born, we were never really encouraged to do so; which I think is why so many people feel unhappy and unfulfilled.

"So, first you've got to find your gift. Then, it's also important that you find a mentor who is aligned with who you really are; one who's going to encourage you to be that person. Because a lot of people want a mentor to learn how to make more money.

But I can tell you right now that this is the wrong approach.

"Because in reality, money is just a by-product of doing meaningful things. So, don't follow the money. Follow the meaning, find a mentor who's in alignment with who you are as a person, and then allow the money to follow. That would be my advice."

Of course, there's probably a thousand more tactics and strategies you could use to find the right mentor for your needs. My goal with this chapter was not to expose them all, but rather to help you get a better understanding of how all this works.

So, at the end of the day, it's all about building relationships; genuine and fun relationships that you can also learn from. That's the goal. And how exactly do you do that? Well, just be authentic, look for people who are aligned with who you really are as a person, and prove that you can actually bring value to the table.

All in all, it's pretty simple. Focus on these three things, and finding a mentor will never have been easier.

BONUS ANECDOTE WITH PEJMAN GHADIMI

Without any type of formal education or formalized training to back him up, Pejman Ghadimi somehow managed to start his corporate career in banking, where he quickly found a way to build a name for himself. But after a couple of years climbing the corporate ladder and making it all the way up to the VP level, Pejman felt like it was time for him to take on a new challenge.

As a result, the man decided to leverage both his experience and his real estate portfolio to create *VIP Motoring*, *Secret Consulting*, and *Secret Entourage*—the three businesses that he's known for today, which have collectively generated over $40 million in revenue ever since.

In addition, Pejman has also authored multiple books, including his latest bestseller entitled *Third Circle Theory*, which puts forward a unique roadmap to a higher level of self-awareness.

Having successfully built the kind of lifestyle that he had always wanted for himself, Pejman Ghadimi now spends most of his time making a difference in the world, teaching others about the importance of self-awareness, belief, and purpose.

"I think good mentorship should always be free," he admitted. "Coaching, on the other hand, doesn't have to be, because it takes time and efforts. You know, if I spend an hour with you doing coaching, it's an hour that I spend *not* doing something else. Whereas if you just come by my office and hang out with me for a day, it doesn't have to change what I do during that day.

"So, I've had this young gentleman who came to me one day asking for some coaching. And typically, when I ask people what they have to offer in exchange, their answer is always 'I'll work for you for free...' or something like that. It just doesn't really mean anything.

"But for some reason, this kid came up to me and said: 'Listen, I'm a very talented graphic designer. I can redesign a lot of these ads that you do. I can do this for you, I can do that, and here's an example of some of the stuff I've done in the past.'

"He started off by showing me his skill sets, then he offered me some value, saying: 'I would love to design some stuff for you for free, and I would like it if you could maybe give me some advice as I'm undergoing this other startup thing.' He showed me that he had skills that were relevant to what I was doing, so I said yes. That's the perfect example of a win-win situation.

"What's funny is that the guy now works full-time for me as a graphic designer, and he's actually making a few thousands of dollars per month doing that. So, I guess what I'm trying to say is that there's always going to be an opportunity for people who simply ask."

To learn more about Pejman Ghadimi and the *Secret Entourage Academy*, an online community of over 200 mentors in the entrepreneurial field, you can visit his website at [http://secretacademics.com].

Chapter 6

HOW DID YOU FIND YOUR FIRST MENTOR?

To be perfectly honest, I don't think I've ever really asked anyone to mentor me. I mean, it always kind of just happened to me. I would simply meet people, get along with them, and from there our relationship would evolve and sometimes lead to mentorship.

Just like that, it always kind of happened very organically. So, without even realizing it, I was probably doing a few things right already.

In fact, I met my first business mentor when I was just 16. I was looking to get a new car, and for some reason, the salesman and I ended up talking about the automotive blog I was running at the time.

He told me that one of his clients also happened to work in the same field, and even offered to make the introductions. So, we got on the phone, spoke a couple of times, and that's how it all started for me; that's how I found my first mentor.

Now, obviously I'm not suggesting that you go buy a new car and expect to get a free mentor out of the deal. But I guess what I'm trying to say is that you never really know when or where you'll find someone willing to mentor you.

"I've had different influencers at different stages of my life, but I've never really been actively looking for anyone," started Dave Ruel. "For example, when I first got involved in the fitness market, one of my friends was already making six figures a year blogging about fitness. And of course, when I saw that, I wanted to learn how he had done it; so he showed me.

"Then, after I had learned with him for two years, launched my first website and had a little bit of success with it, I felt like it was time for me to take the project to a new level. So, I started following Vince DelMonte—who's now one of my closest buddies.

But at the time, I was looking at him like *'Wow! This guy is on the next level; I need to figure out a way to connect with him...'*

"And I didn't want to just reach out to him by email and be like: 'Hey man, could you teach me something?' Because the truth is; I've never been a big fan of that approach anyway. But when I heard that he had opened a new mastermind, I knew that this had to be my ticket, so I signed up for it. And that's pretty much how I've always rolled.

"You know, I like to surround myself with people who have complementary skill sets; I think that's important. I like to have different go-to guys for different situations; people that are more experienced than me in specific areas and that I can call with specific questions. So, that's usually what I'm looking for when I connect with new mentors and influencers."

In the same vein, Pejman Ghadimi also claims that his strategy was never really to look for a formalized mentorship plan.

"The truth is: I don't think I've ever had a coach or a formal mentor," he said. "I never went to someone asking them to mentor me.

Instead, I've always had people who have shared their experience with me, which is something that I've always taken to heart.

"And therefore, because I was clearly making an effort to use all the resources that they were giving me, and because I was actually applying their advice, I've been lucky enough to receive more and more information from these people.

"Because when you apply the advice you get and you really use it to improve and make a difference in your life, that's when people tend to be more inclined to give you more. So, that's exactly what I did; I found someone I could watch and listen to, I paid close attention to what they had to say, and then I kind of built up from there."

Now, as far as I'm concerned, this is probably one of the most effective ways to get the ball rolling, especially if you have no idea where to start. Just find someone you can watch and learn from, listen carefully to what they have to say, and then start implementing it right away.

Who knows, you might end up being mentored by your own boss!

"As a matter of fact, my first mentor was my boss," added James Arthur Ray. "So that's how I found him; I was blessed to work for him. And somehow, he really taught me a lot about life in general. Meaning that, he didn't do a whole lot of tactics like we talked about earlier, but he did ask a lot of great questions.

"And I think part of what made him such a good mentor is that he really knew how to use what's referred to as the Socratic method—which is basically the ability to ask questions to pull the answers out of somebody instead of just giving them your answers. So, he used this a lot with me, and I think that's why I was able to learn so much from him.

"Because let's face it: if you're my mentor and I ask you questions and you provide me with your answers, then you're the one who owns these answers. But if you know how to ask me the right questions and I come up with my own answers, then they're all mine. And my mentor was incredibly good with that."

Be that as it may, James is definitely right on the fact that bosses can sometimes make great mentors. But have you ever thought about just hiring someone right from the start? As it turns out, that's exactly how Stephanie Nickolich found her first mentor.

"It's pretty simple; I paid for his services," said Stephanie. "I paid several thousands of dollars a month for his expertise, and it made a huge difference in my life. Now, a lot of people say that they don't have the money to do that. Well, let me tell you something; you *will* find the money if it's important enough to you.

"You know, at the time I hired my mentor, I was over a hundred thousand dollars in debt—so I didn't have the money. But I did whatever it took, because I knew that I absolutely needed him in my corner. I knew that I had created this crap load of debt by myself, trying to download every program and take every course—doing everything really but getting the help and the support I needed. And as a result, I was now a hundred thousand dollars in debt with no success. It was time for me to stop making excuses.

"So, I don't care if you have to pay for a coach or a mentor; if that person is worth it, then you better figure out a way to cough up the money and make it happen. Because you know, this whole mentor situation absolutely changed my life. Within two years of starting my business, I'm on track to make $3.2 million this year. Before, I was making maybe $20,000 a year—that's just insane! So, as far as I'm concerned, my mentor was worth his weight in gold.

"Now, how I found him was actually through a three-day conference in South Florida. I was in my previous business at the time, and I had bought the VIP ticket for the event, so I was sitting right in front of the room—there was about a hundred attendees in there for dinner, and a board of maybe ten multi-millionaires.

"And at some point while we were eating, they gave the opportunity to about eight people in the audience to ask a question— that's when I jumped off my chair, went literally in front of the room and said: 'Me! Me! Me!' And guess what; it worked! So, they asked me who I was, what I was doing, and I told them.

"The business I was running at the time was growing, but I didn't feel fulfilled. I *knew* from the inside that I could create massive success; but I had no idea how to connect the dots in order to get there. And people could see that I was full of passion; they could see that I was probably going to be successful at some point in my life. But I was obviously missing some very crucial elements for that.

"So, over the next two days—because it was a three-day conference—three people came up to me and recommended that I speak with certain persons in the industry that they felt could really help me. And my mentor was one of them. So, for the next week, I took action and booked calls with every single one of these people.

"And the moment I got on the phone with him, I could feel his confidence. I could feel that he wasn't going to take my bullshit anymore, and I knew right away that he was the guy I needed in my corner—I think we both knew.

"Now, he usually works with corporations, not individuals. But I guess he saw something in me too. And at that point, I honestly didn't care how much he would charge me, because we both knew that we had to make this relationship happen. I was going to figure out a way, and that's exactly what I did. So, I hired him, and it's been a great journey ever since!"

Of course, I'm a big believer in this idea that if you care enough about something, you'll find a way to make it happen. However, I also know firsthand what it's like to be a teenager with no money whatsoever.

If that's your case, you might want to listen carefully to what Gerard Adams had to say, as he went for a completely different approach—one that won't cost you anything but time.

"I would simply create something of value for them; something that was actually interesting for them," said Gerard. "For example, when I met that first CEO—the one that gave me the lesson on the importance of being prepared—I knew that I wanted to learn about investing and the stock market.

"And I knew that in order for me to find a mentor who understood how to trade stocks, I would need to bring people to me instead of just trying to get out there and find people on different platforms.

"So, I decided to create my own platform—a chatroom, back then—and to market it in a way that would allow it to become a place where a lot of experts would gather and talk about the stocks that they were trading.

"Now, the cool part is that I also integrated a rating system in the platform, something similar to what you would find on eBay or Amazon, going from one to five stars. And based on that, you were able to see who was a better stock picker.

"Then, as the owner of the site, all I had to do was to reach out to the five-star traders listed on the platform and start building a relationship with them. So, that's basically how I found most of my mentors; by creating something of value for them."

Obviously, we've talked about this from the very beginning of the book; providing value will always be a great way to build trust and start a relationship. That's an undeniable fact.

But before we go and wrap up this segment, here's what Doug Sandler wanted to add:

"My dad has certainly been one of my very first mentors," he said. "However, I think we probably run across different mentors in every single phase of our life. And sometimes, we don't even realize that they were mentors until we turn around and see that they've helped us go through a particular phase of our life.

"And it doesn't necessarily have to be a mentor in business. It could be someone who's more of a personal mentor; someone who's going to help you go through a life's challenge.

"So, I think what's important is that every step of the way you understand *who* you're looking for, if that makes any sense. Because if you take a closer look at your surroundings, you'll find that you've probably been around mentors your whole life."

It makes sense. I mean, when you were young, you probably saw your parents as your role models. Then, maybe you got to learn from your first boss or from one of your friends. The point being: chances are that you've probably run across multiple mentors in your life already.

Now, if you really want to take this to the next level and find a business mentor who's going to help you with the specifics of your business—or other project—there's a bunch of things you can do. You could use your skills to create something for them, like Gerard Adams did, or you could simply hire them for their advice, like Stephanie Nickolich did.

Of course, it's totally up to you to pick the strategy that you think is going to work best. But whatever you decide, make sure you apply the tips and advice that we've highlighted in the previous chapter. Along with everything else you've learned in this book so far, this should be more than enough to help you find the right mentor for your needs!

BONUS ANECDOTE WITH GERARD ADAMS

Also known as "The Millennial Mentor," Gerard Adams is one of the cofounders of the online news platform *Elite Daily*. He's a serial entrepreneur, an angel investor and a philanthropist who had already made his way up to becoming a self-made millionaire by the age of 24.

After dropping out of college to pave his own path and pursue what he knew he was truly meant to do, Gerard was told by many that he might not be able to make it on his own. Still, his drive kept him pushing and moving forward despite the odds.

In 2015, the entrepreneur and his two partners sold *Elite Daily*—which now had a readership of over 80 million visitors a month—to a global corporation for $50 million. But after driving exotic cars and traveling first class for a while, Gerard has come to realize that a materially rich life without any purpose or fulfillment was really nothing more than an empty dream.

So, at 31 years old, he's now focusing on showing others how to do what he has done, and how to do it with the right mindset. Whether it's through personalized mentorship, social media content, or through his *Leaders Create Leaders* video series, Gerard Adams has made it his mission to inspire and mentor young entrepreneurs on what it really takes to achieve success.

"I told you that in order to find a mentor who really understood how to trade stocks, I had created a forum where investors could gather and exchange about all the stocks that they were trading," said Gerard. "Well, that was a pretty good way to get attention.

"Another thing I did is that I built *Elite Daily*. And already at the time, Ryan Blair was someone that I really admired. I mean, I had read his book and all, but I could also relate to him because of the way he grew up. And I really felt like I wanted to have him as a mentor.

"So, I reached out to him via email, and to provide value, I said: *'Hey, I have this website that I've built from the ground up, and I would love to have an interview with you. If you agree, I will help you get additional exposure for your book and make sales to all of my network. Could you please do me a favor and set up an interview with me? I would love to meet you.'*

"And by doing this, I finally got a response from him. So, I made the investment to meet with him in person, we shot this amazing video interview, and then I did everything I could to promote it in a way that would make a difference for him. From there, we started building a relationship together, I got to ask him questions, and he eventually turned into an investor of mine!"

If you would like to learn more about Gerard Adams and his *Leaders Create Leaders* video series, feel free to check out his website at [http://gerardadams.com].

BONUS INTERVIEW WITH CALEB MADDIX

At 14 years old, Caleb Maddix has already published and sold thousands of copies of his first book: *Keys to Success for Kids*. Not only that, but he's also the CEO of a six-figure company called *Kids 4 Success*, proving to the entire world that age is really nothing but a number.

Now traveling the world to speak with people like Gary Vaynerchuk, Kevin Harrington, John Lee Dumas, Grant Cardone and Darren Hardy, Caleb has become nothing short of a worldwide sensation. Also known for shocking audiences with his poise on stage, the young entrepreneur has been voted one of the top 20 most motivational influencers of 2016.

In addition, Caleb has also been interviewed by *Forbes Magazine*, *The Huffington Post*, and many other major media outlets, inspiring millions of people all around the world to change their mindset and create the life of their dreams.

So, as you would imagine, as soon as I heard about this guy, I absolutely had to figure out a way to ask him a few questions. And while it is true that he may be younger than most of us, it's also fair to say that we probably all have something to learn from him.

WHAT WOULD YOUR DEFINITION OF A MENTOR BE?

"To me, a mentor would be somebody who has more experience than you in a certain area, and who agrees to share that experience with you," started Caleb. "Because you know, we all learn through experience; that's just how our brain is wired.

"However, what most people don't know is that it doesn't necessarily have to be *our* personal experience. In other words, we can also learn through the experience of others.

"So, I think that's basically what a mentor is; somebody who can teach you something that's going to benefit you based upon their experience. That way, you don't have to make the same mistakes that they've made."

WHAT ROLE HAVE YOUR MENTORS PLAYED IN YOUR CAREER?

"They've played a tremendous role. I mean, I've probably saved myself from having my face fall flat on the ground several times because of my mentors; especially since I'm younger.

"You know, there was some decisions that I was going to make, and then I listened to what my dad had to say, I called Grant Cardone and Kevin Harrington, and it turned out that they all disagreed with the decisions I wanted to make. So, I followed their advice, and that's literally what made the difference between my business failing and my business succeeding.

"So, they've helped a lot as far as that goes. And here's the deal; a lot of people think that mentors are people that you have to know personally and call every other week. But in reality, a mentor is a person that can teach you something—now, you don't have to personally know somebody for them to teach you something.

"That's the beauty of 2016; there's a ton of books, YouTube videos and blog posts out there that you can learn from. I mean, if a six-year-old wants to learn how to play piano, he can just go online and study it. So, I think all of that combined has saved me a lot of headaches."

WHAT IS THE BEST ADVICE THAT YOU'VE EVER GOTTEN FROM ONE OF YOUR MENTORS?

"Believe it or not, I've received amazing advice from billionaires, athletes, and all these great people. But the best advice I've ever gotten actually came from a security guard. I was sitting in the hot tub with my dad, and the security guard happened to walk by. So, I asked him how he was doing, we ended up talking about his story, and he said this quote that has literally changed my life. He said: *'Don't sweat the small stuff, because everything is small stuff.'*

"And for some reason, that really resonated with me. Because we tend to always worry about what's going to happen here and there. But the truth is: when you look at the big picture, all these little things are just small stuff. And when you're going to take your last breath, most of these things won't matter at all.

"So, don't sweat the small stuff, because everything is small stuff. That's the best advice I've ever gotten."

HOW DO YOU THINK A MENTOR CAN HELP YOU FULFILL YOUR DREAMS?

"Well, I think mentors can do a lot of things to help you fulfill your dreams. Like I said, they can help you get there faster by sharing their knowledge with you—and a lot of times, they've already done what your trying to do, so they can definitely help you with that.

"They can also provide you with some of the connections that you need. I mean, without all the connections that I've gotten from my mentors, I can confidently say that I would be nowhere near where I am today.

"So, whether it's by sharing their knowledge and their connections with you, or even just by being there to support you whenever you're going through a tough time, a mentor can definitely help you fulfill your dreams."

WHAT WOULD BE YOUR ADVICE TO SOMEONE LOOKING FOR A MENTOR?

"The first thing I would say is; be impressive. Because you know, most mentors are going to be high-level—you don't want a mentor who thinks and acts low-level. That being said, chances are that they're not going to be impressed with you sending them a message or going up to them at a conference asking them to be your mentor— they get that all the time.

"You'd be shocked to see the amount of Facebook messages I get from people asking me to be their mentor. And frankly, I just ignore most of them, because I'm not impressed. So, my first advice would be to do something extreme to get the mentor's attention.

"Then, I would suggest that you do something *for* them as well. In other words, think about how you could give back to them in some way; provide value. That's going to help you a lot.

"And finally, try to apply the advice you get within the first 48 hours—even if it doesn't seem like much at first. Because here's what I've learned; too many people go through the trouble of finding a mentor and asking for these great pieces of advice only to end up never applying them. And the truth is; they're never going to get their big transformation, because information alone does not equal transformation. Information plus application equals transformation.

"So, get your advice, make sure you apply it within the first 48 hours, and then message the person to let them know that you've started implementing it. Because when a mentor sees that you're actually applying their advice, then it becomes very inspiring and fulfilling for them to give you more and more."

HOW DID YOU FIND YOUR FIRST MENTOR?

"Well, I was actually raised by my first mentor; my dad. But aside from that, I would say that my first baseball coach was also one of my first mentors.

"And I remember one day, I was doing tryouts for his team; there was like seven other coaches and a bunch of other kids around, and my dad told me to pick one coach and make it my priority to just go out there and ask him questions.

"So, I literally went up to this man named Coach Schwartz—who's now a coach and mentor for me in business, since he's an absolute genius in business as well—and I just started to ask him questions about my batting form and all that stuff. And although I was young, I really had this hunger to learn and improve my skills. So, he would tell me something, and I would literally go right up to the plate and fix it.

"Now, I was the shortest kid on the team—and probably the worst kid as well— but because of that, because of what I had done, I was the first to be drafted that year.

"And I asked him a couple of years later why he had picked me that day even though I was probably the worst player on the team, and he said: '*Well, I've seen a lot of these other kids out there. And a hundred of them were probably better than you, but you were the most coachable.*'

"So, that's the reason why he picked me; because someone who's willing to learn and apply what they learn is always going to go further than someone who just relies on their talent."

BONUS ANECDOTE

"If you've ever been to St. Petersburg, there's this place called the Station House where you can go to get some work done and meet new people. And one day, as I was there getting some work done, this guy walked up to me and said: 'Oh my gosh! You're Caleb Maddix!'

"So, we talked for a little while, we took a picture together, and as he was leaving, he told me that he was actually hosting this crowdfunding event for Kevin Harrington later that day. And he said that I should swing by if I had a chance.

"Now, I had like four meetings scheduled in the meantime, but I still managed to get there on time. So, I walked in the room and Kevin Harrington was right there, surrounded by six really big guys. And at first I thought maybe I should just leave. But then I remembered a rule that I had learned from Grant Cardone—which is the 1, 2, 3 rule.

"So, I counted to three and I walked right through the six guys. I introduced myself to

Kevin, I talked a bit about what I was doing, and then I said: 'What would be your best advice for me?'

"He gave me some really good advice; I asked him another question, we talked for a bit and that was it. He was really impressed with me.

"And later that night, as I walked out the door, I saw him about to get in his car. So, I just ran up to him, shook his hand and said: 'What would stop you from getting a 15-minute Starbucks with me so I can ask you a couple more questions?' And at that point, he really appreciated the hustle, so he looked at me and said: 'You know what, I'll do you one better. Instead of getting a Star-bucks, come to my house, and we'll do a 30-minute interview on my show if you want.'

"So, that's pretty much how it went. We did the interview, he absolutely loved me, we spoke a couple of times on stage togeth-er, he then invited me to his house again, we talked about my business, and he loved it so much that he actually ended up investing in it!"

To learn more about Caleb Maddix and find out how you can get a free copy of his bestselling book *Keys to Success for Kids*, visit [http://mathieufortintv.com/maddix].

BONUS INTERVIEW WITH SANDY FORSTER

Sandy Forster is an international mentor and an award-winning business owner who has also written and contributed to over eleven bestselling books, including her own bestseller *How to Be Wildly Wealthy FAST*. And after completely transforming her life from welfare to millionaire in just a few short years, she is now teaching others how they can also create their own success.

Using the power of the subconscious mind and other practical strategies to create wealth and abundance in her life, Sandy has gone from being over $100,000 in debt to becoming what she now refers to as a *Wildly Wealthy Woman*.

From her days as a sole parent struggling to raise two young children, she has experienced a complete turnaround, creating over $1.2 million in revenue in less than 12 months.

As a result, Sandy is now recognized as one of the top 50 motivators and prosperity experts in the world. She has won multiple awards, including a *Stevie Award for Women in Business* in 2008, and she has made it a personal mission to help make the world a better place by sharing the principles of creating a life filled with abundance and happiness.

Something you probably don't know is that ever since I started my entrepreneurial journey a couple of years ago, Sandy has always been a great inspiration to me. In fact, she's part of the reason why I started my business in the first place!

So, here's the best part of our conversation. Make sure you take notes!

WHAT WOULD YOUR DEFINITION OF A MENTOR BE?

"Well, for me, a mentor is really someone who has already achieved the success that you want to achieve," stated Sandy. "It's someone who's able to actually show you the way, and maybe show you the shortcuts and the steps you can take, so that you don't have to go out there and try to figure it all out on your own.

"And I know in the older days a mentor was seen as this old retired man who had been in the corporate world and had had great success—you know, the experienced man who was taking this young person under his wing to meet with them every week for an hour or so. But that's not what I believe a mentor is today.

"I believe it's really anyone who has created huge success, and who can basically show you how to follow their footsteps. A mentor is someone who can guide you; someone who can also inspire you and allow you to not have to do it all on your own."

WHAT ROLE HAVE YOUR MENTORS PLAYED IN YOUR CAREER?

"They've played a massive role. And initially, it was very hard for me to reach out to people and connect with them, simply because I was in Australia and most people I looked up to were in America. And when I was first starting out, I couldn't afford to hire someone to be my mentor.

"So, I started following their home-study courses, the teleseminars that they were doing, their audio programs; everything that would help me tap into their wisdom without necessarily having them there to answer my questions. But that alone has made such a massive difference to me as a person and as an entrepreneur, because it allowed me to get really inspired by what other people had achieved.

"And then, when I finally got in a position where I was able to physically meet with people all over the world, again, it made such a massive difference. Because as I said; having a mentor means that you don't have to go out there and make all the mistakes yourself. You don't have to go out there and spend all the time, the energy and the money. It allows you to kind of bypass all that and speed up your way to success."

WHAT IS THE BEST ADVICE THAT YOU'VE EVER GOTTEN FROM ONE OF YOUR MENTORS?

"I think it was to use my book as a big business card. That has literally changed everything for me and my business. Because I'm consistently giving people additional free stuff throughout my book now, whether it's free tips to create more prosperity, free guided visualizations, or even free money magnetizing ideas. But to get those freebies, the readers have to come back to my website and put in their name and email address.

"So, my book really has become my big business card. And the truth is, I've probably given away more books that I've even sold, because I know that once people read the book and they love the material that's in it, they'll definitely come back to my site. So, that's very much how I've grown my business in the recent years; by using my book as a big business card."

HOW DO YOU THINK A MENTOR CAN HELP YOU FULFILL YOUR DREAMS?

"As I've said before, I think it's mostly about the shortcuts. It's about you not having to waste as much time, energy and money on making mistakes, because you're basically following the mentor's footsteps.

"But for me personally, it's also about the inspiration. It's about understanding that everyone who has ever created success started out exactly like you and me. I mean, we knew nothing and we had nothing; no followers, no likes, no nothing. We were just like everyone else, but we took one step after the other and made it happen. And that's what a mentor shows you; that they were just like you, but they kept on going and never gave up.

"And too many people give up. They read the books, go to the seminars, get inspired, but when they start taking action and things don't go as they should—which happens all the time in business—they give up. So, it's those of us who keep going and persist that end up creating the success. And I think that's what most of the mentors I've ever learned from have shown me."

WHAT WOULD BE YOUR ADVICE TO SOMEONE LOOKING FOR A MENTOR?

"First of all, get very clear on what you want to achieve. Because once you're clear on what you want to achieve, then it's just a matter of looking out there and seeing who has achieved that already. And when you're looking at all these potential mentors, you should really focus on who you resonate with the most. Because to me, a mentor is not just someone who's clever and smart; it's also someone that you really feel aligned with and could easily be friends with.

"So, I would recommend that you find a person that really lights you up form the inside out whenever you think about connecting with them and applying their steps. That's going to allow you to attract the circumstances, the people and the opportunities that you truly resonate with."

HOW DID YOU FIND YOUR FIRST MENTOR?

"Actually, my first mentor was Mark Victor Hansen. And honestly, I have no idea how I found him! I mean, I'm way out here in Australia, and this was way before the internet was saturated with everyone; so when you think about it, it doesn't really make any sense. But somehow, I got on an email list and I ended up going to an event of his, and that was it; I was hooked.

"Because when I saw him up on stage, he was literally all over the place—he kept jumping from one thing to the other, and I started thinking: 'Oh my gosh! This man is just a male version of me!' So, if he was able to create success—and by then, he had already created massive success with the *Chicken Soup for the Soul* series—I knew I could do it too.

"And that was a game changer for me, because at that time, I thought that in order to be successful, you had to be this very organized, logical and business-focused person. And he was the complete opposite of that; he was just all about thinking big, getting empowered, getting excited and getting inspired.

"So, that really tipped me over the edge and allowed me to dream bigger and believe that it was all possible. And the belief is what makes it all happen in the long run. So, once I had that belief, then all sorts of amazing things started to happen in my life."

BONUS ANECDOTE

"One of the things I loved about my journey with Mark is that at one point we actually went on a safari in Africa. And it was literally the best business holiday ever. I mean, it was supposed to be more of an adventure holiday, but imagine spending seven hours a day in a minivan with Mark Victor Hansen; you see all the elephants, the lions, and everything, but then, you also get to talk business with Mark. So, this was definitely one of the most amazing holidays/business adventures that I've ever had.

"Now, another thing I really loved was his live events. He doesn't have them anymore, which is sad, but he used to have these great events two or three times a year, where people from all over the world would get together and network with each other.

"And for some reason, he always used to call me up on stage to ask me questions about my experience learning with him and connecting with him. And I remember one time he called me up, and at the next break, this woman came up to me and said: 'Hey Sandy! I'm the person from the email!'

"And I get millions of emails, but this one was special. Here's what happened; one day, I was sitting at my desk, looking at the sun shining through the palm trees outside, and an order came in from someone in Iceland. And I thought this was pretty cool, so I sent the person back an email—which I never do when someone orders—with a picture of my view, saying: 'Hey! Thank you so much for your order! Here's a picture of my morning... Hope you're having a great day!'

"So, it turned out that she was actually the woman I had sent the picture to! And seeing this made me realize just how amazing it was that a mentor could bring together all these people from all around the world and make them connect like that."

To learn more about Sandy Forster and download her free *Prosperity Package* that's going to help you create a life filled with abundance, prosperity, success and happiness, you can visit her website at [http://wildlywealthywomen.com].

FIVE STEPS YOU SHOULD TAKE RIGHT NOW TO GET THE BALL ROLLING

1. WRITE DOWN A LIST OF POTENTIAL MENTORS

Start thinking about who you want to learn from. It could be a well-known entrepreneur, some politician, or even a neighbor. Write down all the names of the people you think are aligned with you, your goals and your vision.

2. TACKLE SOCIAL MEDIA

We've seen that finding the right mentor is all about building the right relationships. And with social media, we are blessed to live in an era where building relationships is now easier than ever. In fact, social media is where I first got in touch with most of my own mentors. So, start engaging with the people you've listed in the previous step. Comment on their posts, ask them questions, watch their videos; you never know where this is going to lead you.

3. GO TO LOCAL EVENTS

Of course, social media isn't everything; a good handshake never gets old. That said, local events can be great for making new connections within your industry. Who knows; maybe you'll meet someone there who can make introductions for you! So, this month, set your intentions right and go to at least one local networking event.

4. ATTRACT MENTORS BY CREATING SOMETHING OF VALUE

We've talked about this a lot throughout the book. Regardless of the situation, one of the most effective ways to get noticed is by providing value. So, instead of wondering how a mentor could benefit you, start focusing on how *your* skills could benefit *them*. On a piece of paper, write down at least three things you could do for each person you've listed in step one.

5. STOP WAITING AND GET GOING WITH YOUR PROJECTS

Again, mentors aren't going to do the work for you. They're looking for people who can make things happen on their own. So, whatever it is that you want to achieve, you might as well just get started right now. Be resourceful, set goals and get things done.

ABOUT THE AUTHOR

MATHIEU FORTIN is a young author and entrepreneur. As a teenager, while most of his friends were doing homework and playing video games, Mathieu was already onto something else; reading everything he could find on business and personal growth.

By the age of 16, he had already launched his first online business, showing the world what a passion, a dream and a vision can accomplish when put altogether. Through the years, Mathieu has been involved in many different projects, going all the way from the automotive industry to the personal development field.

Today, he is focused on one thing; sharing the valuable knowledge he has learned over the past five years from his mentors and his own experiences to help young aspiring entrepreneurs turn their wildest dreams into reality.

FOR MORE INFORMATION:

Website: [http://MathieuFortinTV.com]
Facebook: [https://facebook.com/MathieuFortinTV]
Instagram: [https://instagram.com/MathieuFortinTV]
Twitter: [https://twitter.com/MathieuFortinTV]
Snapchat: [https://snapchat.com/add/mathieu_fortin]
YouTube: [https://youtube.com/MathieuFortinTV]

ACKNOWLEDGMENTS

First, to my amazing guests, Gerard Adams, Sandy Forster, Pejman Ghadimi, Caleb Maddix, Stephanie Nickolich, James Arthur Ray, Dave Ruel and Doug Sandler, I want to say thank you for your generosity and your trust. Working with you on this project has truly been a blessing.

I also want to thank my parents and my friends for being so supportive throughout this journey. The book wouldn't have been possible without you all.

BIOGRAPHIES

GERARD ADAMS

Also known as "The Millennial Mentor," Gerard Adams is one of the cofounders of the online news platform *Elite Daily*. He's a serial entrepreneur, an angel investor and a philanthropist who had already made his way up to becoming a self-made millionaire by the age of 24.

After dropping out of college to pave his own path and pursue what he knew he was truly meant to do, Gerard was told by many that he might not be able to make it on his own. Still, his drive kept him pushing and moving forward despite the odds.

In 2015, the entrepreneur and his two partners sold *Elite Daily*—which now had a readership of over 80 million visitors a month—to a global corporation for $50 million. But after driving exotic cars and traveling first class for a while, Gerard has come to realize that a materially rich life without any purpose or fulfillment was really nothing more than an empty dream.

So, at 31 years old, he's now focusing on showing others how to do what he has done, and how to do it with the right mindset. Whether it's through personalized mentorship, social media content, or through his *Leaders Create Leaders* video series, Gerard Adams has made it his mission to inspire and mentor young entrepreneurs on what it really takes to achieve success.

FOR MORE INFORMATION:

Website: [http://gerardadams.com]
Facebook: [https://facebook.com/gerardadamstv]
Instagram: [https://instagram.com/gerardadams]
Snapchat: [https://snapchat.com/add/hellogerard]
YouTube: [https://youtube.com/GerardAdamsTV]

SANDY FORSTER

Sandy Forster is an international mentor and an award-winning business owner who has also written and contributed to over eleven bestselling books, including her own bestseller *How to Be Wildly Wealthy FAST*.

And after completely transforming her life from welfare to millionaire in just a few short years, she is now teaching others how they can also create their own success.

Using the power of the subconscious mind and other practical strategies to create wealth and abundance in her life, Sandy has gone from being over $100,000 in debt to becoming what she now refers to as a *Wildly Wealthy Woman.*

From her days as a sole parent struggling to raise two young children, she has experienced a complete turnaround, creating over $1.2 million in revenue in less than 12 months.

As a result, Sandy is now recognized as one of the top 50 motivators and prosperity experts in the world. She has won multiple awards, including a *Stevie Award for Women in Business* in 2008, and she has made it a personal mission to help make the world a better place by sharing the principles of creating a life filled with abundance and happiness.

To download Sandy's free *Prosperity Package* and learn how you can create a life filled with abundance and happiness, visit [http://wildlywealthywomen.com].

FOR MORE INFORMATION:

Website: [http://wildlywealthywomen.com]
Facebook: [https://facebook.com/SandyForsterFan]
Instagram: [https://instagram.com/wildlywealthy]

PEJMAN GHADIMI

Without any type of formal education or formalized training to back him up, Pejman Ghadimi somehow managed to start his corporate career in banking, where he quickly found a way to build a name for himself. But after a couple of years climbing the corporate ladder and making it all the way up to the VP level, Pejman felt like it was time for him to take on a new challenge.

As a result, the man decided to leverage both his experience and his real estate portfolio to create *VIP Motoring*, *Secret Consulting*, and *Secret Entourage*—the three businesses that he's known for today, which have collectively generated over $40 million in revenue ever since.

In addition, Pejman has also authored multiple books, including his latest bestseller entitled *Third Circle Theory*, which puts forward a unique roadmap to a higher level of self-awareness.

Having successfully built the kind of lifestyle that he had always wanted for himself, Pejman Ghadimi now spends most of his time making a difference in the world, teaching others about the importance of self-awareness, belief, and purpose.

To learn more about the *Secret Entourage Academy*, a community of over 200 mentors in the entrepreneurial field, you can visit [http://secretacademics.com].

FOR MORE INFORMATION:

Website: [http://pejmanghadimi.com]
Facebook: [https://facebook.com/secretentourage]
Instagram: [https://instagram.com/icreatemillionaires]
Snapchat: [https://snapchat.com/add/se_official]
YouTube: [https://youtube.com/SecretEntourage]

CALEB MADDIX

At 14 years old, Caleb Maddix has already published and sold thousands of copies of his first book: *Keys to Success for Kids*. Not only that, but he's also the CEO of a six-figure company called *Kids 4 Success*, proving to the entire world that age is really nothing but a number.

Now traveling the world to speak with people like Gary Vaynerchuk, Kevin Harrington, John Lee Dumas, Grant Cardone and Darren Hardy, Caleb has become nothing short of a worldwide sensation. Also known for shocking audiences with his poise on stage, the young entrepreneur has been voted one of the top 20 most motivational influencers of 2016.

In addition, Caleb has also been interviewed by *Forbes Magazine*, *The Huffington Post*, and many other major media outlets, inspiring millions of people all around the world to change their mindset and create the life of their dreams.

To download your free copy of Caleb's bestselling book *Keys to Success for Kids*, visit [http://mathieufortintv.com/maddix].

FOR MORE INFORMATION:

Website: [http://kids4success.tv]
Facebook: [https://facebook.com/calebmaddix]
Instagram: [https://instagram.com/calebmaddix]
Snapchat: [https://snapchat.com/add/calebmaddix13]
Twitter: [https://twitter.com/CalebMaddix]

STEPHANIE NICKOLICH

Stephanie Nickolich—also known as the "Millionista Mentor"—is a thriving entrepreneur known for helping other women crush their doubts, master what she calls their "money mindset" and capitalize on their strengths to skyrocket their success.

After making heads turn for the first time as a sales strategist in the corporate world, where she helped building a $1.2 million company in just a year's time, Stephanie left her job to create the e-commerce empire *Accessory Fanatic*, where she ended up getting her first real taste of entrepreneurial success.

Looking for a way to make a positive impact in the world, she then created *Success Society,* an online community where women in business can connect, collaborate and capitalize on their dreams. As a result, Stephanie now uses her fun and outspoken approach to inspire, empower and educate businesswomen worldwide—but most importantly, she's doing what she loves!

FOR MORE INFORMATION:

Website: [http://stephanienickolich.com]
Facebook: [https://facebook.com/styleyoursuccess]
Twitter: [https://twitter.com/StephNickolich]

JAMES ARTHUR RAY

James Arthur Ray is a *New York Times* bestselling author who is also known for his success in the business world. In fact, his former company was featured on the *Inc. 500* list in 2009 as one of the fastest growing privately held companies in the United States.

But after rising to the top of his industry, the man literally lost everything he had in the same year—from the business that took him 20 years to build to his entire life savings, his home, his reputation and ultimately, his liberty.

Today, however, the man claims that the experience of losing everything has actually allowed him to realize quite a few things, including the fact that anyone can turn their entire life around by learning how to make adversity an ally.

James is also one of the coauthors of *The Secret*, a feature-length film and *New York Times* bestseller on its own, and has been featured many times on national TV shows, like *The Oprah Winfrey Show*, *Good Morning America*, *The Today Show*, *Piers Morgan Live* and *CNN's Larry King Live*.

To download James Arthur Ray's free guide to find your purpose and turn your life around, visit [http://jamesray.com/living-on-purpose-survey].

FOR MORE INFORMATION:

Website: [http://jamesray.com]
Facebook: [https://facebook.com/officialjamesarthurray]
Twitter: [https://twitter.com/JamesARay]

DAVE RUEL

Dave Ruel is a serial entrepreneur and former bodybuilder who's been featured in just about every major fitness magazine you can imagine. His golden ticket? The *Anabolic Cooking* cookbook.

And although he has been quite successful over the past few years as an entrepreneur, it wasn't always like that. As a kid, the serial entrepreneur wasn't really good at school. It's only later on that his passion for fitness and bodybuilding led him to come up with his own recipes for healthy and tasty muscle-building meals—which he then decided to sell online.

As a result, ever since he started doing business online in 2007, Dave Ruel has made over $16 million in various fields—including publishing, nutrition, personal growth and business coaching. Today, the man spends most of his time traveling the world to make a difference in people's lives and help them grow their own businesses.

FOR MORE INFORMATION:

Website: [http://daveruel.com]
Facebook: [https://facebook.com/daveruel]
Instagram: [https://instagram.com/daveruel]

DOUG SANDLER

With over 30 years of business experience as an entrepreneur, a business owner, a manager and a staff member, Doug Sandler is the author of *Nice Guys Finish First*, which came out in 2015 and quickly became a #1 ranked Amazon bestseller.

His expertise revolves around making connections, building relationships and strengthening bonds both inside and outside organizations. However, don't let the "Mr. Nice Guy" tag mislead you, as Doug has entered into many high level negotiations and is known to be anything but a pushover.

The speaking and consulting business he has built over the past few years is geared towards both improving relationships and winning business through his time-tested sales, service and relationship building system. So, not only is Doug Sandler a nationally recognized speaker, but his podcast, *The Nice Guys on Business*, is also one of the top business podcasts out there.

As a result, Doug has been titled by a leading social media marketing company as one of the top 100 Social Media Influencers to follow.

FOR MORE INFORMATION:

Website: [http://dougsandler.com]
Facebook: [https://facebook.com/dasandler]
Twitter: [https://twitter.com/djdoug]

www.ingramcontent.com/pod-product-compliance
Lightning Source LLC
LaVergne TN
LVHW051348080426
835509LV00020BA/3343